Step-by-Step, Practical Recipes Chocolate

Cakes & Traybakes

For a special occasion, or even just a treat, try an indulgent chocolate cake or traybake to be shared amongst friends.

Puddings

Delicious combinations of chocolate and other flavours create wholesome puddings.

Tarts

Chocolate is the perfect ingredient to turn any tart into an irresistible dessert.

FLAME TREE has been creating family-friendly, classic and beginner recipes for our bestselling cookbooks for over 20 years now. Our mission is to offer you a wide range of expert-tested dishes, while providing clear images of the final dish so that you can match it to your own results. We hope you enjoy this super selection of recipes – there are plenty more to try! Titles in this series include:

**Cupcakes • Slow Cooker • Curries
Soups & Starters • Baking & Breads
Cooking on a Budget • Winter Warmers
Party Cakes • Meat Eats • Party Food
Chocolate • Sweet Treats**

www.flametreepublishing.com

Sachertorte

INGREDIENTS

Cuts into 10–12 slices

150 g/5 oz plain dark chocolate

150 g/5 oz unsalted butter, softened

125 g/4 oz caster sugar, plus
  2 tbsp

3 medium eggs, separated

150 g/5 oz plain flour, sifted

To decorate:

225 g/8 oz apricot jam

125 g/4 oz plain dark
  chocolate, chopped

125 g/4 oz unsalted butter

25 g/1 oz milk chocolate

FOOD FACT

In 1832, the Viennese foreign minister asked a Vienna hotel to prepare an especially tempting cake. The head pastry chef was ill and so the task fell to second-year apprentice, Franz Sacher, who presented this delightful cake.

1 Preheat the oven to 180°C/350°F/Gas Mark 4, 10 minutes before baking. Lightly oil and line a deep 23 cm/9 inch cake tin.

2 Melt the 150 g/5 oz of chocolate in a heatproof bowl set over a pan of simmering water. Stir in 1 tablespoon of water and leave to cool.

3 Beat the butter and 125 g/4 oz of the sugar together until light and fluffy. Beat in the egg yolks, one at a time, beating well between each addition. Stir in the melted chocolate, then the flour.

4 In a clean grease-free bowl, whisk the egg whites until stiff peaks form, then whisk in the remaining sugar. Fold into the chocolate mixture and spoon into the prepared tin. Bake in the preheated oven for 30 minutes until firm. Leave for 5 minutes, then turn out onto a wire rack to cool. Leave the cake upside down.

5 To decorate the cake, split the cold cake in 2 and place one half on a serving plate. Heat the jam and rub through a fine sieve.

6 Spread half the jam onto the first cake half, then cover with the remaining cake layer and spread over the remaining jam. Leave at room temperature for 1 hour or until the jam has set.

7 Place the plain dark chocolate with the butter into a heatproof bowl set over a saucepan of simmering water and heat until the chocolate has melted. Stir until smooth, then leave until thickened. Use to cover the cake.

8 Melt the milk chocolate in a heatproof bowl set over a saucepan of simmering water. Place in a small greaseproof piping bag and snip a small hole at the tip. Pipe Sacher with a large 'S' on the top. Leave to set at room temperature.

3

4

5

White Chocolate & Raspberry Mousse Gateau

INGREDIENTS

Cuts into 8 slices

4 medium eggs
125 g/4 oz caster sugar
75 g/3 oz plain flour, sifted
25 g/1 oz cornflour, sifted
3 gelatine leaves
450 g/1 lb raspberries, thawed
  if frozen
400 g/14 oz white chocolate
200 g/7 oz plain fromage frais
2 medium egg whites
25 g/1 oz caster sugar
4 tbsp raspberry or orange liqueur
200 ml/7 fl oz double cream
fresh raspberries, halved, to decorate

HELPFUL HINT

Do not try to wrap the chocolate-covered parchment around the cake before it is nearly set or it will run down and be uneven.

1 Preheat the oven to 190°C/375°F/Gas Mark 5, 10 minutes before baking. Oil and line 2 x 23 cm/9 inch cake tins. Whisk the eggs and sugar until thick and creamy and the whisk leaves a trail in the mixture. Fold in the flour and cornflour, then divide between the tins. Bake in the preheated oven for 12–15 minutes or until risen and firm. Cool in the tins, then turn out onto wire racks.

2 Place the gelatine with 4 tablespoons of cold water in a dish and leave to soften for 5 minutes. Purée half the raspberries, press through a sieve, then heat until nearly boiling. Squeeze out excess water from the gelatine, add to the purée and stir until dissolved. Reserve.

3 Melt 175 g/6 oz of the chocolate in a bowl set over a saucepan of simmering water. Leave to cool, then stir in the fromage frais and purée. Whisk the egg whites until stiff and whisk in the sugar. Fold into the raspberry mixture with the rest of the raspberries.

4 Line the sides of a 23 cm/9 inch springform tin with nonstick baking parchment. Place 1 layer of sponge in the base and sprinkle with half the liqueur. Pour in the raspberry mixture and top with the second sponge. Brush with the remaining liqueur. Press down and chill in the refrigerator for 4 hours. Unmould onto a plate.

5 Cut a strip of double thickness nonstick baking parchment to fit around the cake and stand 1 cm/½ inch higher. Melt the remaining white chocolate and spread thickly onto the parchment. Leave until just setting. Wrap around the cake and freeze for 15 minutes. Peel away the parchment. Whip the cream until thick and spread over the top. Decorate with raspberries.

1

2

4

French Chocolate Pecan Torte

INGREDIENTS

Cuts into 16 slices

200 g/7 oz plain dark
   chocolate, chopped

150 g/5 oz butter, diced

4 large eggs

100 g/3½ oz caster sugar

2 tsp vanilla essence

125 g/4 oz pecans, finely ground

2 tsp ground cinnamon

24 pecan halves, lightly toasted,
   to decorate

For the chocolate glaze:

125 g/4 oz plain dark
   chocolate, chopped

60 g/2½ oz butter, diced

2 tbsp clear honey

¼ tsp ground cinnamon

FOOD FACT

Although this recipe is French, the torte actually originates from Germany, and tends to be a very rich cake-like dessert. It is delicious served with a fruity mixed berry compote.

1 Preheat the oven to 180°C/350°F/Gas Mark 4, 10 minutes before baking. Lightly butter and line a 20.5 x 5 cm/8 x 2 inch springform tin with nonstick baking paper. Wrap the tin in a large sheet of tinfoil to prevent water seeping in.

2 Melt the chocolate and butter in a saucepan over a low heat and stir until smooth. Remove from the heat and cool.

3 Using an electric whisk, beat the eggs, sugar and vanilla essence until light and foamy. Gradually beat in the melted chocolate, ground nuts and cinnamon, then pour into the prepared tin.

4 Set the foil-wrapped tin in a large roasting tin and pour in enough boiling water to come 2 cm/¾ inches up the sides of the tin. Bake in the preheated oven until the edge is set, but the centre is still soft when the tin is gently shaken. Remove from the oven and place on a wire rack to cool.

5 For the glaze, melt all the ingredients over a low heat until melted and smooth, then remove from the heat. Dip each pecan halfway into the glaze and set on a sheet of nonstick baking paper until set. Allow the remaining glaze to thicken slightly.

6 Remove the cake from the tin and invert. Pour the glaze over the cake smoothing the top and spreading the glaze around the sides. Arrange the glazed pecans around the edge of the torte. Allow to set and serve.

3

4

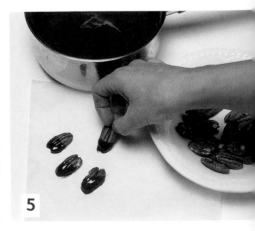

5

Chocolate Fudge Brownies

INGREDIENTS

Makes 16

125 g/4 oz butter

175 g/6 oz plain dark chocolate,
   roughly chopped or broken

225 g/8 oz caster sugar

2 tsp vanilla essence

2 medium eggs, lightly beaten

150 g/5 oz plain flour

175 g/6 oz icing sugar

2 tbsp cocoa powder

15 g/ ½ oz butter

FOOD FACT

Chocolate is obtained from the bean of the cacao tree and was introduced to Europe in the 16th century. It is available in many different forms, from cocoa powder to couverture, which is the best chocolate to use for cooking, as it has a high cocoa butter content and melts very smoothly.

1 Preheat the oven to 180°C/350°F/Gas Mark 4, 10 minutes before baking. Lightly oil and line a 20.5 cm/8 inch square cake tin with greaseproof or baking paper.

2 Slowly melt the butter and chocolate together in a heatproof bowl set over a saucepan of simmering water. Transfer the mixture to a large bowl.

3 Stir in the sugar and vanilla essence, then stir in the eggs. Sift over the flour and fold together well with a metal spoon or rubber spatula. Pour into the prepared tin.

4 Transfer to the preheated oven and bake for 30 minutes until just set. Remove the cooked mixture from the oven and leave to cool in the tin before turning it out on to a wire rack.

5 Sift the icing sugar and cocoa powder into a small bowl and make a well in the centre.

6 Place the butter in the well then gradually add about 2 tablespoons of hot water. Mix to form a smooth, spreadable icing.

7 Pour the icing over the cooked mixture. Allow the icing to set before cutting into squares. Serve the brownies when they are cold.

2

3

5

Chocolate Nut Brownies

INGREDIENTS

Makes 16

125 g/4 oz butter

150 g/5 oz soft light brown sugar, firmly packed

50 g/2 oz plain dark chocolate, roughly chopped or broken

2 tbsp smooth peanut butter

2 medium eggs

50 g/2 oz unsalted roasted peanuts, finely chopped

100 g/3½ oz self-raising flour

For the topping:

125 g/4 oz plain dark chocolate, roughly chopped or broken

50 ml/2 fl oz sour cream

TASTY TIP

For those with a really sweet tooth, replace the plain dark chocolate used for the topping with white chocolate. As with plain dark chocolate, buy a good quality white chocolate and take care when melting; it burns very easily, especially in the microwave.

1 Preheat the oven to 180°C/350°F/Gas Mark 4, 10 minutes before baking. Lightly oil and line a 20.5 cm/8 inch square cake tin with greaseproof or baking paper.

2 Combine the butter, sugar and chocolate in a small saucepan and heat gently until the sugar and chocolate have melted, stirring constantly. Reserve and cool slightly.

3 Mix together the peanut butter, eggs and peanuts in a large bowl.

4 Stir in the cooled chocolate mixture. Sift in the flour and fold together with a metal spoon or rubber spatula until combined.

5 Pour into the prepared tin and bake in the preheated oven for about 30 minutes, or until just firm.

6 Cool for 5 minutes in the tin before turning out on to a wire rack to cool.

7 To make the topping, melt the chocolate in a heatproof bowl over a saucepan of simmering water, making sure that the base of the bowl does not touch the water.

8 Cool slightly, then stir in the sour cream until smooth and glossy. Spread over the brownies, refrigerate until set, then cut into squares. Serve the brownies cold.

Rich Devil's Food Cake

INGREDIENTS

Cuts into 12–16 slices

450 g/1 lb plain flour
1 tbsp bicarbonate of soda
½ tsp salt
75 g/3 oz cocoa powder
300 ml/ ½ pint milk
150 g/5 oz butter, softened
400 g/14 oz soft dark brown sugar
2 tsp vanilla essence
4 large eggs

For the chocolate fudge frosting:

275 g/10 oz caster sugar
½ tsp salt
125 g/4 oz plain dark
  chocolate, chopped
225 ml/8 fl oz milk
2 tbsp golden syrup
125 g/4 oz butter, diced
2 tsp vanilla essence

1 Preheat the oven to 180°C/350°F/Gas Mark 4, 10 minutes before baking. Lightly oil and line the bases of three 23 cm/9 inch cake tins with greaseproof or baking paper. Sift the flour, bicarbonate of soda and salt into a bowl.

2 Sift the cocoa powder into another bowl and gradually whisk in a little of the milk to form a paste. Continue whisking in the milk until a smooth mixture results.

3 Beat the butter, sugar and vanilla essence until light and fluffy then gradually beat in the eggs, beating well after each addition. Stir in the flour and cocoa mixtures alternately in three or four batches.

4 Divide the mixture evenly among the three tins, smoothing the surfaces evenly. Bake in the preheated oven for 25–35 minutes, until cooked and firm to the touch. Remove, cool and turn out on to a wire rack. Discard the lining paper.

5 To make the frosting, put the sugar, salt and chocolate into a heavy-based saucepan and stir in the milk until blended. Add the golden syrup and butter. Bring the mixture to the boil over a medium-high heat, stirring to help dissolve the sugar.

6 Boil for 1 minute, stirring constantly. Remove from the heat, stir in the vanilla essence and cool. When cool, whisk until thickened and slightly lightened in colour.

7 Sandwich the three cake layers together with about a third of the frosting, placing the third cake layer with the flat side up. Transfer the cake to a serving plate and, using a metal palette knife, spread the remaining frosting over the top and sides. Swirl the top to create a decorative effect and serve.

2

5

7

Chocolate Mousse Cake

INGREDIENTS

Cuts into 8–10 servings

For the cake:
450 g/1 lb plain dark
   chocolate, chopped
125 g/4 oz butter, softened
3 tbsp brandy
9 large eggs, separated
150 g/5 oz caster sugar

For the chocolate glaze:
225 ml/8 fl oz double cream
225 g/8 oz plain dark
   chocolate, chopped
2 tbsp brandy
1 tbsp single cream and white
   chocolate curls, to decorate

FOOD FACT

Wonderfully rich and delicious served with a fruity compote – why not try making cherry compote using either fresh, if in season or otherwise tinned in fruit juice. Stone the cherries, or drain, and then simmer on a low heat with a little apple juice until reduced.

1 Preheat the oven to 180°C/350°F/Gas Mark 4, 10 minutes before baking. Lightly oil and line the bases of two 20.5 cm/8 inch springform tins with baking paper. Melt the chocolate and butter in a bowl set over a saucepan of simmering water. Stir until smooth. Remove from the heat and stir in the brandy.

2 Whisk the egg yolks and the sugar, reserving 2 tablespoons of the sugar, until thick and creamy. Slowly beat in the chocolate mixture until smooth and well blended. Whisk the egg whites until soft peaks form, then sprinkle over the remaining sugar and continue whisking until stiff but not dry.

3 Fold a large spoonful of the egg whites into the chocolate mixture. Gently fold in the remaining egg whites. Divide about two-thirds of the mixture evenly between the tins, tapping to distribute the mixture evenly. Reserve the remaining one-third of the chocolate mousse mixture for the filling. Bake in the preheated oven for about 20 minutes, or until the cakes are well risen and set. Remove and cool for at least 1 hour.

4 Loosen the edges of the cake layers with a knife. Using your fingertips, lightly press the crusty edges down. Pour the rest of the mousse over one layer, spreading until even. Carefully unclip the side, remove the other cake from the tin and gently invert on to the mousse, bottom side up to make a flat top layer. Discard lining paper and chill for 4–6 hours, or until set.

5 To make the glaze, melt the cream and chocolate with the brandy in a heavy-based saucepan and stir until smooth. Cool until thickened. Unclip the side of the mousse cake and place on a wire rack. Pour over half the glaze and spread to cover. Allow to set, then decorate with chocolate curls and the remaining glaze.

Chocolate Pear Pudding

INGREDIENTS

Serves 6

140 g/4½ oz butter, softened

2 tbsp soft brown sugar

400 g can of pear halves, drained and
juice reserved

25 g/1 oz walnut halves

125 g/4 oz golden caster sugar

2 medium eggs, beaten

75 g/3 oz self-raising flour, sifted

50 g/2 oz cocoa powder

1 tsp baking powder

prepared chocolate custard, to serve

HELPFUL HINT

To soften butter or margarine quickly, pour hot water in a mixing bowl to warm, leave for a few minutes, then drain and dry. Cut the butter or margarine into small pieces and leave at room temperature for a short time. Do not attempt to melt in the microwave as this will make the fat oily and affect the texture of the finished cake.

1 Preheat the oven to 190°C/375°F/Gas Mark 5, 10 minutes before baking. Butter a 20.5 cm/8 inch sandwich tin with 15 g/½ oz of the butter and sprinkle the base with the soft brown sugar. Arrange the drained pear halves on top of the sugar, cut-side down. Fill the spaces between the pears with the walnut halves, flat-side upwards.

2 Cream the remaining butter with the caster sugar then gradually beat in the beaten eggs, adding 1 tablespoon of the flour after each addition. When all the eggs have been added, stir in the remaining flour.

3 Sift the cocoa powder and baking powder together, then stir into the creamed mixture with 1–2 tablespoons of the reserved pear juice to give a smooth dropping consistency.

4 Spoon the mixture over the pear halves, smoothing the surface. Bake in the preheated oven for 20–25 minutes, or until well risen and the surface springs back when lightly pressed.

5 Remove from the oven and leave to cool for 5 minutes. Using a palate knife, loosen the sides and invert onto a serving plate. Serve with custard.

1

2

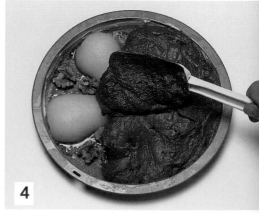
4

Spicy White Chocolate Mousse

INGREDIENTS

Serves 4–6

6 cardamom pods

125 ml/4 fl oz milk

3 bay leaves

200 g/7 oz white chocolate

300 ml/½ pint double cream

3 medium egg whites

1–2 tsp cocoa powder, sifted,
  for dusting

1 Tap the cardamom pods lightly so they split. Remove the seeds, then, using a pestle and mortar, crush lightly. Pour the milk into a small saucepan and add the crushed seeds and the bay leaves. Bring to the boil gently over a medium heat. Remove from the heat, cover and leave in a warm place for at least 30 minutes to infuse.

2 Break the chocolate into small pieces and place in a heatproof bowl set over a saucepan of gently simmering water. Ensure the water is not touching the base of the bowl. When the chocolate has melted remove the bowl from the heat and stir until smooth.

3 Whip the cream until it has slightly thickened and holds its shape, but does not form peaks. Reserve. Whisk the egg whites in a clean, grease-free bowl until stiff and standing in soft peaks.

4 Strain the milk through a sieve into the cooled, melted chocolate and beat until smooth. Spoon the chocolate mixture into the egg whites, then using a large metal spoon, fold gently. Add the whipped cream and fold in gently.

5 Spoon into a large serving dish or individual small cups. Chill in the refrigerator for 3–4 hours. Just before serving, dust with a little sifted cocoa powder and then serve.

TASTY TIP

Chocolate and spices go together very well as this recipe demonstrates. White chocolate has an affinity with spices such as cardamom, while dark and milk chocolate go very well with cinnamon.

2

3

4

White Chocolate Trifle

INGREDIENTS

Serves 6

1 homemade or bought chocolate
   Swiss roll, sliced
4 tbsp brandy
2 tbsp Irish cream liqueur
425 g can black cherries, drained
   and pitted, with 3 tbsp of the
   juice reserved
900 ml/1½ pints double cream
125 g/4 oz white chocolate, broken
   into pieces
6 medium egg yolks
50 g/2 oz caster sugar
2 tsp cornflour
1 tsp vanilla essence
50 g/2 oz plain dark chocolate, grated
50 g/2 oz milk chocolate, grated

HELPFUL HINT

It is critical that the custard is not allowed to boil once the eggs have been added. Otherwise, the mixture turns to sweet scrambled eggs and is unusable. Cook over a very gentle heat, stirring constantly and testing the mixture often.

1 Place the Swiss roll slices in the bottom of a trifle dish and pour over the brandy, Irish cream liqueur and a little of the reserved black cherry juice to moisten the Swiss roll. Arrange the black cherries on the top.

2 Pour 600 ml/1 pint of the cream into a saucepan and add the white chocolate. Heat gently to just below simmering point. Whisk together the egg yolks, caster sugar, cornflour and vanilla essence in a small bowl.

3 Gradually whisk the egg mixture into the hot cream, then strain into a clean saucepan and return to the heat.

4 Cook the custard gently, stirring throughout until thick and coats the back of a spoon.

5 Leave the custard to cool slightly, then pour over the trifle. Leave the trifle to chill in the refrigerator for at least 3–4 hours, or preferably overnight.

6 Before serving, lightly whip the remaining cream until soft peaks form, then spoon the cream over the set custard. Using the back of a spoon, swirl the cream in a decorative pattern. Sprinkle with grated plain and milk chocolate and serve.

2

3

5

White Chocolate Eclairs

INGREDIENTS

Serves 4–6

50 g/2 oz unsalted butter
60 g/2½ oz plain flour, sifted
2 medium eggs, lightly beaten
6 ripe passion fruit
300 ml/½ pint double cream
3 tbsp kirsch
1 tbsp icing sugar
125 g/4 oz white chocolate, broken
  into pieces

HELPFUL HINT

Passion fruit are readily available in supermarkets. They are small, round purplish fruits that should have quite wrinkled skins. Smooth passion fruit are not ripe and will have little juice or flavour.

1 Preheat the oven to 190°C/375°F/Gas Mark 5, 10 minutes before baking. Lightly oil a baking sheet. Place the butter and 150 ml/¼ pint of water in a saucepan and gradually bring to the boil.

2 Remove the saucepan from the heat and immediately add the flour all at once, beating with a wooden spoon until the mixture forms a ball in the centre of the saucepan. Leave to cool for 3 minutes.

3 Add the eggs a little at a time, beating well after each addition until the paste is smooth, shiny and of a piping consistency.

4 Spoon the mixture into a piping bag fitted with a plain nozzle. Sprinkle the oiled baking sheet with water. Pipe the mixture onto the baking sheet in 7.5 cm/3 inch lengths.

5 Bake in the preheated oven for 18–20 minutes, or until well risen and golden. Make a slit along the side of each eclair.

6 Return the eclairs to the oven for a further 2 minutes to dry out. Transfer to a wire rack and leave to cool.

7 Halve the passion fruit and scoop the pulp of 4 of the fruits into a bowl. Add the cream, kirsch and icing sugar and whip until the cream holds it shape. Carefully spoon or pipe into the eclairs.

8 Melt the chocolate in a small heatproof bowl set over a saucepan of simmering water and stir until smooth.

9 Leave the chocolate to cool slightly, then spread over the top of the eclairs. Scoop the seeds and pulp out of the remaining passion fruit. Sieve. Use the juice to drizzle around the eclairs when serving.

2

5

7

Chocolate Roulade

INGREDIENTS

Serves 8

150 g/5 oz golden caster sugar
5 medium eggs, separated
50 g/2 oz cocoa powder

For the filling:

300 ml/½ pint double cream
3 tbsp whisky
50 g/2 oz creamed coconut, chilled
2 tbsp icing sugar
coarsely shredded coconut, toasted

1 Preheat the oven to 180°C/350°F/Gas Mark 4, 10 minutes before baking. Oil and line a 33 x 23 cm/13 x 9 inch Swiss roll tin with a single sheet of nonstick baking parchment. Dust a large sheet of baking parchment with 2 tablespoons of the caster sugar.

2 Place the egg yolks in a bowl with the remaining sugar, set over a saucepan of gently simmering water and whisk until pale and thick. Sift the cocoa powder into the mixture and carefully fold in.

3 Whisk the egg whites in a clean, grease-free bowl until soft peaks form. Gently add 1 tablespoon of the whisked egg whites into the chocolate mixture then fold in the remaining whites. Spoon the mixture onto the prepared tin, smoothing the mixture into the corners. Bake in the preheated oven for 20–25 minutes, or until risen and springy to the touch.

4 Turn the cooked roulade out onto the sugar-dusted baking parchment and carefully peel off the lining paper. Cover with a clean damp tea towel and leave to cool.

5 To make the filling, pour the cream and whisky into a bowl and whisk until the cream holds its shape. Grate in the chilled creamed coconut, add the icing sugar and gently stir in. Uncover the roulade and spoon about three-quarters of coconut cream on the roulade and roll up. Spoon the remaining cream on the top and sprinkle with the coconut, then serve.

HELPFUL HINT

Take care when rolling up the roulade in this recipe as it can break up quite easily.

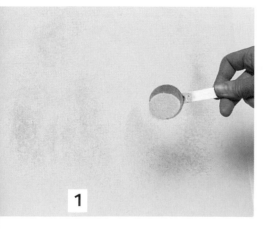

1

3

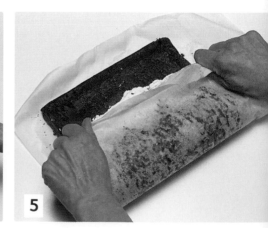

5

Chocolate Meringue Nest with Fruity Filling

INGREDIENTS

Serves 8

125 g/4 oz hazelnuts, toasted

125 g/4 oz golden caster sugar

75 g/3 oz plain dark chocolate, broken
into pieces

2 medium egg whites

pinch of salt

1 tsp cornflour

½ tsp white wine vinegar

chocolate curls, to decorate

For the filling:

150 ml/¼ pint double cream

150 g/5 oz mascarpone cheese

prepared summer fruits, such
as strawberries, raspberries
and redcurrants

HELPFUL HINT

To make chocolate curls, melt the chocolate over hot water then pour onto a cool surface, preferably marble if available. Leave until just set but not hard, then using a large cook's knife or a cheese parer, push the blade at an angle across the surface of the chocolate to form curls.

1 Preheat the oven to 110°C/225°F/Gas Mark 1, 5 minutes before baking and line a baking sheet with nonstick baking parchment. Place the hazelnuts and 2 tablespoons of the caster sugar in a food processor and blend to a powder. Add the chocolate and blend again until the chocolate is roughly chopped.

2 In a clean, grease-free bowl, whisk the egg whites and salt until soft peaks form. Gradually whisk in the remaining sugar a teaspoonful at a time and continue to whisk until the meringue is stiff and shiny. Fold in the cornflour and the white wine vinegar with the chocolate and hazelnut mixture.

3 Spoon the mixture into 8 mounds, about 10 cm/4 inches in diameter, on the baking parchment. Do not worry if not perfect shapes. Make a hollow in each mound, then place in the preheated oven. Cook for 1½ hours, then switch the oven off and leave in the oven until cool.

4 To make the filling, whip the cream until soft peaks form. In another bowl, beat the mascarpone cheese until it is softened, then mix with the cream. Spoon the mixture into the meringue nests and top with the fresh fruits. Decorate with a few chocolate curls and serve.

1

2

3

Double Chocolate Truffle Slice

INGREDIENTS

Cuts into 12–14 slices

1 quantity Chocolate Pastry
  (*see* page 38)
300 ml/½ pint double cream
300 g/11 oz plain dark
  chocolate, chopped
25–40 g/1–1½ oz unsalted
  butter, diced
50 ml/2 fl oz brandy or liqueur
icing sugar or cocoa powder
  for dusting

1 Preheat the oven to 200°C/400°F/Gas Mark 6, 15 minutes before baking. Prepare the chocolate pastry and chill in the refrigerator, according to instructions.

2 Roll the dough out to a rectangle about 38 x 15 cm/15 x 6 inches and use to line a rectangular loose-based flan tin, trim then chill in the refrigerator for 1 hour.

3 Place a sheet of nonstick baking parchment and baking beans in the pastry case, then bake blind in the preheated oven for 20 minutes. Remove the baking parchment and beans and bake for 10 minutes more. Leave to cool completely.

4 Bring the cream to the boil. Remove from the heat and add the chocolate all at once, stirring until melted and smooth. Beat in the butter, then stir in the brandy liqueur. Leave to cool slightly, then pour into the cooked pastry shell. Refrigerate until set.

5 Cut out 2.5 cm/1 inch strips of nonstick baking parchment. Place over the tart in a criss-cross pattern and dust with icing sugar or cocoa.

6 Arrange chocolate leaves, caraque or curls around the edges of the tart. Refrigerate until ready to serve. Leave to soften at room temperature for 15 minutes before serving.

TASTY TIP

Liqueurs that would work very well in this recipe include Tia Maria, Kahlua, Cointreau, Grand Marnier, Amaretto and Crème de Menthe.

2

4

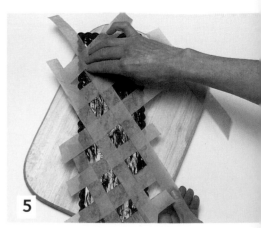

5

Mini Pistachio & Chocolate Strudels

INGREDIENTS

Makes 24

5 large sheets filo pastry
50 g/2 oz butter, melted
1–2 tbsp caster sugar for sprinkling
1 tbsp icing sugar for dusting
50 g/2 oz white chocolate, melted,
  to decorate

For the filling:

125 g/4 oz unsalted pistachios,
  finely chopped
3 tbsp caster sugar
50 g/2 oz plain dark chocolate,
  finely chopped
1–2 tsp rosewater

1 Preheat the oven to 170°C/325°F/Gas Mark 3, 10 minutes before baking. Lightly oil 2 large baking sheets. For the filling, mix the finely chopped pistachio nuts, the sugar and dark chocolate in a bowl. Sprinkle with the rosewater and stir lightly together and reserve.

2 Cut each filo pastry sheet into 4 to make 23 x 18 cm/ 9 x 7 inch rectangles. Place 1 rectangle on the work surface and brush with a little melted butter. Place another rectangle on top and brush with a little more butter. Sprinkle with a little caster sugar and spread about 1 dessertspoon of the filling along one short end. Fold the short end over the filling, then fold in the long edges and roll up. Place on the baking sheet seam-side down. Continue with the remaining pastry sheets and filling until both are used.

3 Brush each strudel with the remaining melted butter and sprinkle with a little caster sugar. Bake in the preheated oven for 20 minutes, or until golden brown and the pastry is crisp.

4 Remove from the oven and leave on the baking sheet for 2 minutes, then transfer to a wire rack. Dust with icing sugar. Place the melted white chocolate in a small piping bag fitted with a plain writing pipe and pipe squiggles over the strudel. Leave to set before serving.

TASTY TIP

Keep the unused filo pastry covered with a clean damp tea towel to prevent it from drying out.

1

2

3

Chocolate Raspberry Mille Feuille

INGREDIENTS

Serves 6

450 g/1 lb puff pastry, thawed
   if frozen
1 quantity Raspberry Chocolate
   Ganache (*see* page 46), chilled
700 g/1½ lbs fresh raspberries, plus
   extra for decorating
icing sugar for dusting

For the raspberry sauce:

225 g/8 oz fresh raspberries
2 tbsp seedless raspberry jam
1–2 tbsp caster sugar, or to taste
2 tbsp lemon juice or
   framboise liqueur

HELPFUL HINT

If you prefer, make 1 big mille feuille by leaving the 3 strips whole in step 2. Slice the finished mille feuille with a sharp serrated knife.

1 Preheat the oven to 200°C/400°F/Gas Mark 6, 15 minutes before baking. Lightly oil a large baking sheet and sprinkle with a little water. Roll out the pastry on a lightly floured surface to a rectangle about 43 x 28 cm/17 x 11 inches. Cut into 3 long strips. Mark each strip crossways at 6.5 cm/2½ inch intervals using a sharp knife; this will make cutting the baked pastry easier and neater. Carefully transfer to the baking sheet, keeping the edges as straight as possible.

2 Bake in the preheated oven for 20 minutes or until well risen and golden brown. Place on a wire rack and leave to cool. Carefully transfer each rectangle to a work surface and, using a sharp knife, trim the long edges straight. Cut along the knife marks to make 18 rectangles.

3 Place all the ingredients for the raspberry sauce in a food processor and blend until smooth. If the purée is too thick, add a little water. Taste and adjust the sweetness if necessary. Strain into a bowl, cover and chill in the refrigerator.

4 Place 1 pastry rectangle on the work surface flat-side down, spread with a little chocolate ganache and sprinkle with a few fresh raspberries. Spread a second rectangle with a little ganache, place over the first, pressing gently, then sprinkle with a few raspberries. Place a third rectangle on top, flat-side up, and spread with a little chocolate ganache.

5 Arrange some raspberries on top and dust lightly with a little icing sugar. Repeat with the remaining pastry rectangles, chocolate ganache and fresh raspberries.

6 Chill in the refrigerator until required and serve with the raspberry sauce and any remaining fresh raspberries.

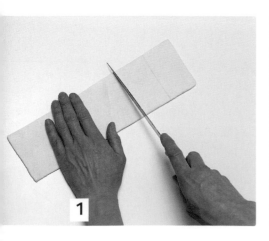

Chocolate & Almond Daquoise with Summer Berries

INGREDIENTS

Serves 8

For the almond meringues:
6 large egg whites
¼ tsp cream of tartar
275 g/10 oz caster sugar
½ tsp almond essence
50 g/2 oz blanched or flaked
  almonds, lightly toasted and
  finely ground

For the chocolate buttercream:
75 g/3 oz butter, softened
450 g/1 lb icing sugar, sifted
50 g/2 oz cocoa powder, sifted
3–4 tbsp milk or single cream
550 g/1¼ lb mixed summer berries
  such as raspberries, strawberries
  and blackberries

To decorate:
toasted flaked almonds
icing sugar

1. Preheat the oven to 140°C/275°F/Gas Mark 1, 10 minutes before baking. Line 3 baking sheets with nonstick baking paper and draw a 20.5 cm/8 inch round on each one.

2. Whisk the egg whites and cream of tartar until soft peaks form. Gradually beat in the sugar, 2 tablespoons at a time, beating well after each addition, until the whites are stiff and glossy.

3. Beat in the almond essence, then using a metal spoon or rubber spatula gently fold in the ground almonds.

4. Divide the mixture evenly between the 3 circles of baking paper, spreading neatly into the rounds and smoothing the tops evenly.

5. Bake in the preheated oven for about 11¼ hours or until crisp, rotating the baking sheets halfway through cooking. Turn off the oven, allow to cool for about 1 hour, then remove and cool completely before discarding the lining paper

6. Beat the butter, icing sugar and cocoa powder until smooth and creamy, adding the milk or cream to form a soft consistency.

7. Reserve about a quarter of the berries to decorate. Spread 1 meringue with a third of the buttercream and top with a third of the remaining berries. Repeat with the other meringue rounds, buttercream and berries.

8. Scatter with the toasted flaked almonds, the reserved berries and sprinkle with icing sugar and serve.

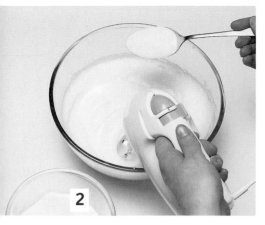

2

6

7

Chocolate, Orange & Pine Nut Tart

INGREDIENTS

Cuts into 8–10 slices

For the sweet shortcrust pastry:

150 g/5 oz plain flour

½ tsp salt

3–4 tbsp icing sugar

125 g/4 oz unsalted butter, diced

2 medium egg yolks, beaten

½ tsp vanilla essence

For the filling:

125 g/4 oz plain dark
   chocolate, chopped

60 g/2½ oz pine nuts,
   lightly toasted

2 large eggs

grated zest of 1 orange

1 tbsp Cointreau

225 ml/8 fl oz whipping cream

2 tbsp orange marmalade

1 Preheat the oven to 200°C/400°F/Gas Mark 6, 15 minutes before baking. Place the flour, salt and sugar in a food processor with the butter and blend briefly. Add the egg yolks, 2 tablespoons of iced water and the vanilla essence and blend until a soft dough is formed. Remove and knead until smooth, wrap in clingfilm and chill in the refrigerator for 1 hour.

2 Lightly oil a 23 cm/9 inch loose-based flan tin. Roll the dough out on a lightly floured surface to a 28 cm/11 inch round and use to line the tin. Press into the sides of the flan tin, crimp the edges, prick the base with a fork and chill in the refrigerator for 1 hour. Bake blind in the preheated oven for 10 minutes. Remove and place on a baking sheet. Reduce the oven temperature to 190°C/375°F/Gas Mark 5.

3 To make the filling, sprinkle the chocolate and the pine nuts evenly over the base of the pastry case. Beat the eggs, orange zest, Cointreau and cream in a bowl until well blended, then pour over the chocolate and pine nuts.

4 Bake in the oven for 30 minutes, or until the pastry is golden and the custard mixture is just set. Transfer to a wire rack to cool slightly. Heat the marmalade with 1 tablespoon of water and brush over the tart. Serve warm or at room temperature.

FOOD FACT

Cointreau is an orange-flavoured liqueur and is used in many recipes. You could substitute Grand Marnier or any other orange liqueur, if you prefer.

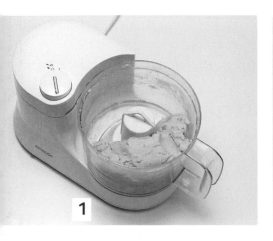

1

2

3

Pear & Chocolate Custard Tart

INGREDIENTS

Cuts into 6–8 slices

For the chocolate pastry:

125 g/4 oz unsalted butter, softened
60 g/2½ oz caster sugar
2 tsp vanilla essence
175 g/6 oz plain flour, sifted
40 g/1½ oz cocoa powder
whipped cream, to serve

For the filling:

125 g/4 oz plain dark
  chocolate, chopped
225 ml/8 fl oz whipping cream
50 g/2 oz caster sugar
1 large egg
1 large egg yolk
1 tbsp crème de cacao
3 ripe pears

HELPFUL HINT

The chocolate pastry is very soft so rolling it between sheets of clingfilm will make it much easier to handle without having to add a lot of extra flour.

1. Preheat the oven to 190°C/375°F/Gas Mark 5, 10 minutes before baking. To make the pastry, put the butter, sugar and vanilla essence into a food processor and blend until creamy. Add the flour and cocoa powder and process until a soft dough forms. Remove the dough, wrap in clingfilm and chill in the refrigerator for at least 1 hour.

2. Roll out the dough between 2 sheets of clingfilm to a 28 cm/11 inch round. Peel off the top sheet of clingfilm and invert the pastry round into a lightly oiled 23 cm/9 inch loose-based flan tin, easing the dough into the base and sides. Prick the base with a fork, then chill in the refrigerator for 1 hour.

3. Place a sheet of nonstick baking parchment and baking beans in the case and bake blind in the oven for 10 minutes. Remove the parchment and beans and bake for a further 5 minutes. Remove and cool.

4. To make the filling, heat the chocolate, cream and half the sugar in a medium saucepan over a low heat, stirring until melted and smooth. Remove from the heat and cool slightly before beating in the egg, egg yolk and crème de cacao. Spread evenly over the pastry case base.

5. Peel the pears, then cut each pear in half and carefully remove the core. Cut each half crossways into thin slices and arrange over the custard, gently fanning the slices towards the centre and pressing into the chocolate custard. Bake in the oven for 10 minutes.

6. Reduce the oven temperature to 180°C/350°F/Gas Mark 4 and sprinkle the surface evenly with the remaining sugar. Bake in the oven for 20–25 minutes, or until the custard is set and the pears are tender and glazed. Remove from the oven and leave to cool slightly. Cut into slices, then serve with spoonfuls of whipped cream.

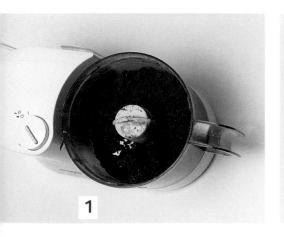

1

2

5

Chocolate Apricot Linzer Torte

INGREDIENTS

Cuts into 10–12 slices

For the chocolate almond pastry:

75 g/3 oz whole blanched almonds
125 g/4 oz caster sugar
215 g/7½ oz plain flour
2 tbsp cocoa powder
1 tsp ground cinnamon
½ tsp salt
grated zest of 1 orange
225 g/8 oz unsalted butter, diced
2–3 tbsp iced water

For the filling:

350 g/12 oz apricot jam
75 g/3 oz milk chocolate, chopped
icing sugar, for dusting

1 Preheat the oven to 375°C/190°F/Gas Mark 5, 10 minutes before baking. Lightly oil a 28 cm/11 inch flan tin. Place the almonds and half the sugar into a food processor and blend until finely ground. Add the remaining sugar, flour, cocoa powder, cinnamon, salt and orange zest and blend again. Add the diced butter and blend in short bursts to form coarse crumbs. Add the water 1 tablespoon at a time until the mixture starts to come together.

2 Turn onto a lightly floured surface and knead lightly, roll out, then using your fingertips, press half the dough onto the base and sides of the tin. Prick the base with a fork and chill in the refrigerator. Roll out the remaining dough between 2 pieces of clingfilm to a 28–30.5 cm/11–12 inch round. Slide the round onto a baking sheet and chill in the refrigerator for 30 minutes.

3 For the filling, spread the apricot jam evenly over the chilled pastry base and sprinkle with the chopped chocolate.

4 Slide the dough round onto a lightly floured surface and peel off the top layer of clingfilm. Using a straight edge, cut the round into 1 cm/½ inch strips; allow to soften until slightly flexible. Place half the strips, about 1 cm/½ inch apart, to create a lattice pattern. Press down on each side of each crossing to accentuate the effect. Press the ends of the strips to the edge, cutting off any excess. Bake in the preheated oven for 35 minutes, or until cooked. Leave to cool before dusting with icing sugar and serve cut into slices.

TASTY TIP

When making the pastry do not allow the dough to form into a ball or it will be tough.

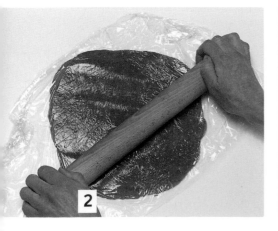

2

3

4

White Chocolate & Macadamia Tartlets

INGREDIENTS

Makes 10

1 quantity Sweet Shortcrust Pastry
  (*see* page 36)
2 medium eggs
50 g/2 oz caster sugar
250 ml/9 fl oz golden syrup
40 g/1½ oz butter, melted
50 ml/2 fl oz whipping cream
1 tsp vanilla or almond essence
225 g/8 oz unsalted macadamia nuts,
  coarsely chopped
150 g/5 oz white chocolate,
  coarsely chopped

1 Preheat the oven to 200°C/400°F/Gas Mark 6, 15 minutes before baking. Roll the pastry out on a lightly floured surface and use to line 10 x 7.5–9 cm/3–3½ inch tartlet tins. Line each tin with a small piece of tinfoil and fill with baking beans. Arrange on a baking sheet and bake blind in the preheated oven for 10 minutes. Remove the tinfoil and baking beans and leave to cool.

2 Beat the eggs with the sugar until light and creamy, then beat in the golden syrup, the butter, cream and vanilla or almond essence. Stir in the macadamia nuts. Sprinkle 100 g/3½ oz of the chopped white chocolate equally over the bases of the tartlet cases and divide the mixture evenly among them.

3 Reduce the oven temperature to 180°C/350°F/Gas Mark 4 and bake the tartlets for 20 minutes, or until the tops are puffy and golden and the filling is set. Remove from the oven and leave to cool on a wire rack.

4 Carefully remove the tartlets from their tins and arrange closely together on the wire rack. Melt the remaining white chocolate and, using a teaspoon or a small paper piping bag, drizzle the melted chocolate over the surface of the tartlets in a zig-zag pattern. Serve slightly warm or at room temperature.

FOOD FACT

Macadamia nuts come from Hawaii and are large, crisp, buttery flavoured nuts. They are readily available from supermarkets.

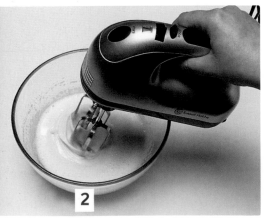

2

2

4

Chocolate Lemon Tartlets

INGREDIENTS

Makes 10

1 quantity Chocolate Pastry
  (*see* page 38)
175 ml/6 fl oz double cream
175 g/6 oz plain dark
  chocolate, chopped
2 tbsp butter, diced
1 tsp vanilla essence
350 g/12 oz lemon curd
225 ml/8 fl oz prepared custard sauce
225 ml/8 fl oz single cream
½ –1 tsp almond essence

To decorate:
grated chocolate
toasted flaked almonds

TASTY TIP

Lemon curd is very easy to make. In a medium-sized heatproof bowl, mix together 175 g/6 oz of caster sugar, the grated rind and juice of 2 large lemons and 4 large eggs. Add 125 g/4 oz cubed unsalted butter and place the bowl over a saucepan of gently simmering water. Stir often until thickened, about 20 minutes. Leave to cool and use as above.

1 Preheat the oven to 200°C/400°F/Gas Mark 6, 15 minutes before baking. Roll the prepared pastry out on a lightly floured surface and use to line 10 x 7.5 cm/3 inch tartlet tins. Place a small piece of crumpled tinfoil in each and bake blind in the preheated oven for 12 minutes. Remove from the oven and leave to cool.

2 Bring the cream to the boil, then remove from the heat and add the chocolate all at once. Stir until smooth and melted. Beat in the butter and vanilla essence and pour into the tartlets and leave to cool.

3 Beat the lemon curd until soft and spoon a thick layer over the chocolate in each tartlet, spreading gently to the edges. Do not chill in the refrigerator or the chocolate will be too firm.

4 Place the prepared custard sauce into a large bowl and gradually whisk in the cream and almond essence until the custard is smooth and runny.

5 To serve, spoon a little custard onto a plate and place a tartlet in the centre. Sprinkle with grated chocolate and almonds, then serve.

1

2

3

Raspberry Chocolate Ganache & Berry Tartlets

INGREDIENTS

Makes 10

1 quantity Chocolate Pastry
(*see* page 38)
600 ml/1 pint whipping cream
275 g/10 oz seedless raspberry jam
225 g/8 oz plain dark chocolate,
   chopped
700 g/1½ lb raspberries or other
   summer berries
50 ml/2 fl oz framboise liqueur
1 tbsp caster sugar
crème fraîche, to serve

1 Preheat the oven to 200°C/400°F/Gas Mark 6, 15 minutes before cooking. Make the chocolate pastry and use to line 8 x 7.5 cm/3 inch tartlet tins. Bake blind in the preheated oven for 12 minutes.

2 Place 400 ml/14 fl oz of the cream and half of the raspberry jam in a saucepan and bring to the boil, whisking constantly to dissolve the jam. Remove from the heat and add the chocolate all at once, stirring until the chocolate has melted.

3 Pour into the pastry-lined tartlet tins, shaking gently to distribute the ganache evenly. Chill in the refrigerator for 1 hour or until set.

4 Place the berries in a large shallow bowl. Heat the remaining raspberry jam with half the framboise liqueur over a medium heat until melted and bubbling. Drizzle over the berries and toss gently to coat.

5 Divide the berries among the tartlets, piling them up if necessary. Chill in the refrigerator until ready to serve.

6 Remove the tartlets from the refrigerator for at least 30 minutes before serving. Using an electric whisk, whisk the remaining cream with the caster sugar and the remaining framboise liqueur until it is thick and softly peaking. Serve with the tartlets and crème fraîche.

1

2

3

Step-by-Step, Practical Recipes Chocolate: Tips & Hints

Helpful Hint

To avoid the occurrence of splitting when melting chocolate, chop the bar into small pieces first. You should keep the chocolate away from excessively high heat. If placed in a bowl over a pan of boiling water, be careful not to let the water touch the bottom of the bowl and never allow any steam or water to come into contact with the chocolate. If using the microwave, set the temperature to low and heat in short bursts, stirring in between. Only heat chocolate in a pan on direct heat if another liquid is being mixed in simultaneously. If the chocolate splits it can be rescued by stirring in 1 tbsp vegetable oil until its glossy smoothness returns.

Food Fact

When the Spanish brought the cocoa bean home they also brought the word 'cocao' as well. In every other European country it is still known as cocao – it is only in English that it is known as cocoa.

Helpful Hint

When grating chocolate, grate onto a piece of nonstick baking parchment using the coarse side of a box grater. It is then easier to sprinkle onto the top of cakes, puddings and tarts from the paper rather than using your fingers.

Tasty Tip

White chocolate is available in bars as well as in chips. As there are no cocoa solids in white chocolate, look for one with a good percentage of cocoa butter, as it is the cocoa butter that gives the chocolate its luscious, creamy texture.

Helpful Hint

All ovens vary, so it is important to be aware of this when baking. Always check the dish about 10 minutes before the end of the recommended cooking time. If cooked, remove the dish and make a note by the recipe. This is especially important if cooking with a fan oven as they cook between 10–20 degrees hotter than conventional ovens. Most chocolate desserts and cakes are best if cooked in the centre of the oven in the middle of the shelf.

Tasty Tip

If a chocolate recipe includes gelatine, there is no need to panic as it is very easy to use. Simply soak sheet gelatine in cold water until softened and then squeeze out the excess liquid. The gelatine should then be added to hot liquid, where it will melt on contact and help the mixture to set.

Helpful Hint

Chocolate is sensitive to strong light or temperature changes, and can absorb strong odours. Accordingly, it is best to store chocolate in a cool, dry place away from direct sunlight; although it is best not to store chocolate in the refrigerator. If chocolate gets too hot, the cocoa butter will naturally rise to the surface which gives a greying colour and a white coating. This change in appearance is not dangerous and the chocolate can still be eaten or used in cooking, although the flavour may be slightly affected.

Tasty Tip

Chocolate shapes can be an excellent way to decorate your chocolate desserts and cakes. To make chocolate shapes, simply spoon melted chocolate into a piping bag and pipe onto waxed paper in whatever shape you like – hearts and stars are simple designs which also look great. Place the waxed paper sheet flat in the refrigerator until fully set and then peel off the shapes and place in position on your dessert.

Food Fact

Dark chocolate contains more cocoa solids than milk chocolate or white chocolate, and its lower sugar content and higher antioxidant count make it more healthy. It may be particularly beneficial in reducing blood pressure and the risk of heart disease as it encourages healthy blood flow which can help prevent the blocking of arteries.

Food Fact

Although cocoa trees can live for up to 200 years, they can take some five years to produce their first beans and usually only produce high quality cocoa beans for a 25 year span. The latin translation for cocoa tree is *Theobroma Cacao*, which means 'food of the gods'.

First published in 2013 by
FLAME TREE PUBLISHING LTD
Crabtree Hall, Crabtree Lane, Fulham,
London, SW6 6TY, United Kingdom
www.flametreepublishing.com

NOTE: Recipes using uncooked eggs should be avoided by infants, the elderly, pregnant women and anyone suffering from an illness.

18 17 16 15 14 13   10 9 8 7 6 5 4 3 2 1

ISBN: 978-0-85775-854-5

ACKNOWLEDGEMENTS: Authors: Catherine Atkinson, Juliet Barker, Gina Steer, Vicki Smallwood, Carol Tennant, Mari Mererid Williams, Elizabeth Wolf-Cohen and Simone Wright. Photography: Colin Bowling, Paul Forrester and Stephen Brayne. Home Economists and Stylists: Jacqueline Bellefontaine, Mandy Phipps, Vicki Smallwood and Penny Stephens. Some props supplied by Barbara Stewart at Surfaces. Publisher and Creative Director: Nick Wells. Editorial: Catherine Taylor, Laura Bulbeck, Esme Chapman, Emma Chafer, Gina Steer and Karen Fitzpatrick. Design and Production: Chris Herbert, Mike Spender and Helen Wall.